The Night the Moon Went Sailing

Poems by Dan Close

ONION
RIVER

PRESS

Burlington, Vermont

Sailing Moon, Bears, Coyotes, Panthers, The Beaver, and *Bees* appeared in the anthology *Windblown*, Writing the Land and Vermont Land Trust, November 2022.

Garth the Big was included in the anthology *Writing the Land Northeast*, Writing the Land and Vermont Land Trust, 2021.

Cicada, Voyage, A Medieval Song of Southern France, and *The Saco At Dahl's Reserve* appeared in various issues of *The Mountain Troubadour*, a publication of The Poetry Society of Vermont.

Bright Star and *What the Abenaki Say About Dogs* appeared in *What the Abenaki Say About Dogs – Poems and Stories of Lake Champlain*, Tamarac Press, Warren, Vermont 2009.

Onion River Press
24 Maple Street, Suite 214
Burlington, VT 05401
info@onionriverpress.com

ISBN: 978-1-957184-26-5
Library of Congress Control Number: 2023904409

for Joanie

Contents

Part 1
Sailing Moon
and other celestial objects

Sailing Moon

The night the moon went sailing across the azure sky,
Ah! Well do I remember the pumpkin in its eye –
'twas the brightest moon forever that was seen by you or I,
The night the moon went sailing across the azure sky...

This Night So Dark

This night so dark I cannot see your face
This moonless night, without a trace of light except for stars

Where and why do the wild geese fly
When all is dark in the nighttime sky?

Orion with his sword and shield
strides toward the zenith

pushing the red-eyed Taurean
into the West.

Visionary

Starship
      Spaceship
            Space dust
Small as a mote
      that swings through morning light
            through the shaft of sunlight
that stands like a diagonal column in the young one's bedroom...

The boy watches the vagrant mote
      concentrating on its wonderment,
            transfixed.

The worried mother, appearing at the doorway of the room,
      "What are you looking at?"
'What can he be looking at? Is he all right? Is he strange?'
      "What are you looking at?"

"Little pieces of light," not moving his eyes.
      "Little pieces of light that move by themselves.
            What are they?"

"Dust," she sighs. "Just dust," she smiles, relieved.

"They're pretty," says the baby boy. "How do they move?
      How do they fly?"

"On the air..."

The young boy stands transfixed and stares.
Motes of dust in a fresh morning room
      full of the sun and bright, scarce-moving air.

Spacedust.

Always with us.

The starship spreads its wings –
the dark light of deep space
glints off its shields of black-streaked heavy-plated gold.
it roars its fire-foaming life across the galaxy,
leaves a trail of being,
molecules, so wide apart out here, disturbed anyway.

It rockets like an old god's arrow
        through soundless space

Intent on unseen stars.
        Far away.
                Far over the curve...

"What are you looking at?
        What do you see that I cannot?
What do you look at that I cannot see that you are seeing?"

Past the sun, past the suns, beyond the Milky Way,
Past the star, past the stars,
Beyond the furthest fringe
        of the wheel of the spinning galaxy,

Spindrift
        Stardrift
                Spacedust

"Beyond all galaxies
        I watch the curve –
I watch the curve where space and time
        never seem to really, truly, meet.
I watch that space unfold Infinity."

The Night Is Sitting

The night is sitting
in clouds of mist,
in skeins of drizzle,
Ancient fishnets set to trap

the solitary walker

with just a touch enough of wind
to make the cold air sting,
to make the throat go raw,
and give him not a place to go but tears —

The old abrasive word-wounds running dry.

Skylarkin'

The shadow that walks
my computer screen
seems happy here in the
middle of the night,
enthralled as it is
by the light of the world
reflected from the screen-saver pic
of Cayuga Lake.
It savors the reflected light
much as I do the
Globed Google Earth.

For both of us
a universe of reflected gladness
a grand and glorious
playground
on which we gambol
the hours away
awe-struck by
the beauty of it all.
He with an unknown purpose,
I with – the unknown.

The Nature of Things

Who knows if somewhere deep inside of every one of us
On some deep-hidden atom of our pancreas or spleen,
Some Newton or an Einstein sits in contemplation
And wonders if all things are relative,
       or even if all things are what they seem,
And whether if his planet is all headed right
And wonders on the nature of the Thing.

Supposin'

Supposing God needs spectacles
And supposing you're a fly
And he swats you off the table
And you die
And He looks down,
Says "Aw, I thought you were
      a piece of dust. I'm sorry."

Meanwhile, you're lying there dead,
Wings broken, legs cracked,
And the Old Man's remorse
Lives on in His mind
And you're done.
      What then?

Fragile places abound;
This universe lives on in instability.

Who set it up this way?
And which direction is the original Eden now?

Angels

Angels dwell in planes of light
Which is why we cannot see 'em
We all look for colors bright
Instead of auras in between 'em.

While we look both high and low
Angels on a path they know
Flit to left and fly to right
From early dawn to candlelight.

And then when we look right to left
They turn at angles uncomputable
They take off on a soaring flight
Straight into realms so strange and beautiful

We cannot follow with our eyes,
Much less our minds. That's no surprise.
But that's a fact that's undisputable.

Part 2
Frost

Frost

Frost didn't write too much, considering.
Mostly he farmed
and taught
and muttered to himself about all the energy he wasted.
Some mutterings of his soul
take hold in us
and stay.

Frost's Mountain

The mountain was his lodestone; his magic;
and like a special hidden power
he never mentioned it but once
except obliquely
by inference.
The purple mountain,
he called it
and only once he wrote its name that I could find
and never wrote its poem.

...the mist cascading down the mountain
But frozen into place in the glacier-gouged ravine
there on the north face
placed there by the gods for us to see, if gods
be glaciers from 20,000 years ago,
if glaciers be gods from old Norse legends of sea-mist
and dragon-ship...

He was, after all, just a man
not a legend, not then.
That would be for later
His face more chiseled later
For now, face rugged, craggy yet to come,
Not Hawthorne's poet –
Well, perhaps he was
But not the legend yet.
Strange, though, he never wrote
About the great range
to the south.
North of Boston it was indeed,
and he north of it. Now,
that's a piece far north
more than most would like to travel.

Days, nights, winters, summers
he stuck it out
longer than any of them
and the great range gave him scraps of poems.
He never wrote them down.

...there is a strangeness there
It is a living thing
Nothing to do with us
No matter how we look at it...

He bought the farmhouse for the mountain.
That was that. All there was to it.
Price doubled? Paid, without a murmur,
Then set to work, to farm, to clear the spring.
Emerging in the early morning sun, he'd heave a sigh,
Look south down to that mist-filled valley
Between the two containing mountains of the notch.

How much it must have stymied him,
Beguiled him, conquered him.
How much Hawthorne must have troubled him
As he nibbled round the edges of that old man's work.
What caused *that* work to work?

So. A sigh, a tightened belt, a grab for the axe
Off to work on kindling for the winter
To better the size of the woodpile
While shattering logs of cordwood into kindling.

Feeling the warmth of the day as it slipped by in morning hours,
Back on the porch, stupefied and satisfied with work,
Another look at the monster blue mountain.
A snort, and the sound of the screen door slamming shut.
His wife, jumping a little, wondering at
His frame of mind this day.

Anger was his, and would remain so.
But he was there this day to recognize the thing
brought on by that hill – that damned hill –
that stood and mocked him and his powers.

"Why?" he would ask his farmer neighbor
(The two of them heaving rocks back on the ancient common wall
one by one.)
"Why" he would say, "does that old pile of rocks
down there stand winter's blasts so well?
Why doesn't it collapse into its notch and fill it up?"

"Tried it wonct," said the neighbor. "Still see the scar.
Notch is bigger than you'd 'spect." Then after resting,
Sighing, gazing off with hands on hips, "Come on, Robert,
Let's get this last big one up top. Robert? You there?"

Robert smiled, put away the thoughts and concepts
Of the great blue mountain for the smaller greatness of
The flat granite stone that stood between them,
Then letting out his breath in one big whooshing sigh
Bent down and grasped that rock on his side,
Neighbor on his, together they lifted, placed it,
Set it stone on stone, looked at it through sweaty
Eyes, then at each other, much as to say "Okay by you?"

"Until this time next year," said the neighbor,
finally, grinning.
That satisfied Robert, who, turning, waved, said
"Next year, then."

Laughing at himself in his foolishness about time and his mountain both,
he turned and went back home. His tussle with the hill could wait.
If that great blue hulk thought it had all the patience in the world,
He would show it he had some piece of patience too.

Perhaps, he thought, he was not yet the man
                    to match the mountain,
           but he would take some thing out of this day –
           his work, alongside of his farmer neighbor.
He would use that, stone for stone, and see
                    what that would build,
And wait to see what that big old blue mountain
           had in store for him.

He grimaced with the hurt both in his back and mind,
And went back home to work his poetry again.

And he would hone his patience with the mountain,
And work on that piece in some distant future time,
           hazed over for now,
But still the gem was there, he knew.

He would have patience for that poem to come to light,
And when it did, he would be waiting for it,
And take it by the neck, or wing,
And wrestle it to the ground.

The afternoon was growing dim
When he sat down at his old desk,
His mind set on stone, but not in stone.
It was still agile, even at this time of day, he figured,
And he commenced to write.

Frost's Pasture in Franconia

Mushrooms coming
Forest going
Meadow back again

Burst trees lie shattered
By winter's early winds

Farm field
Pasture
Forest back again

Bayberry
Aster
In the lateness of the day
In the darkness of the sky

Behind the barn; behind the house,
A scruffy walkway waits for chiseled poetry.

I saw the sign point to the left,
So I walked right
(You're trespassing, you know)
Well, he was, too,
Trespassing on the earth –
Took it for what it was,
Went on
After he had had a miner's say.

More of a pilgrim than a seer, I.

Him too, but having the Gift.
He knowing that, too.
Said it when asked,

"I guess I just had more of nature
                than the rest."
Nothing but the truth, there,
And here the place he found it –
One of them, at least.
For over ten years he worked this place
That overlooked the Ranges to the south.
"North Of Boston", indeed!
North of the Ranges, he might have said
But it wouldn't have had the same cachet
Or sale-ability. Oh, he knew that part, too,
Canny old man turned brittle with farms.

Frost's Farmhouse, Late October

Visitors and pilgrims –
Just enough of us
To keep the place alive
For just one day

And space and time
Enough to stay apart
To give each other time
To grasp the place
Each in his or her own way.

Dave's Instructions On Painting
An Acrylic Drip of Robert Frost

"You've got to know when to stop.
Stop! You've got him! Stop!
No! No! You've gone too far!"
Too many lines now in that ancient weathered face.
"Try again, but this time, make it spare."
Good advice from a poet of the brush
to a poet of the pen.

Lines Written At Frost's Farm In November

The gloomiest day of the latest weekend of the fall
Loved by the looming mountains or by none at all.
The rainbow of leaves blown away and gone,
The brown and ashen trees turn toward their
       winter coats of tightened grey.
No snap to this air, more of a just plain chill
Takes us to the cliff of winter's coming
     and bids us ill.

Saved by the fire, saved by the wood
Sawn and split in the sweetest days of the latest spring,
Aged in the summer sun, now put to use,
Covers us over with summer warmth, this last year's wood,
As snow will soon cover the fields and the roof.

Now is the time of hunkering down,
Of bitterness, forgetful of beauty,
Time of starkness and interminable waiting
For lilac time to come again next spring,
With a new forest of wood to cut and split,
To start fresh, and to live.

Mist

People don't show up out of the
mist anymore
Like they used to do in old
Frost poems...
No tramps in mudtime
No hired hands come home
to the only home they'd ever known

No, now is all brightness and light
except in our muddled minds,
fit for the fire, if nothing else

Still striving for some
other kind of light
Still wondering what in the world
the world is for
Where it is going and why
And if we're going along
with it
Or going to be left behind.

And what that means
Drives a quandary into our hearts
Much like an old woodsplitter
shatters a block of wood
and turns it into kindling.

Part 3

On The Heights

In The Golden Dragon Restaurant In New York

In the Golden Dragon Restaurant on 55th Street,
Surrounded by La Caravelle, La Cote Basque, La Piscine Expensif,
And too many other eating places too numerous to mention,
Seated at a table at the far back,
Old Li Po snaps green beans.
It is between mealtimes, three p. m.
Even in Manhattan not many customers are here.
It is the time to snap green beans,
To twist dumpling dough,
To prepare for the evening meal.
So Li Po snaps green beans,
Snapping them with a metal snipper
To keep from bruising them;
To keep them fresh and new.

Across the table from him sits Song Ling.
Young with beauty, fresh off the boat from Hong Kong,
She deftly twists dumpling dough around fresh ground pork centers.
She waits on tables, too, in this off-hour.
"Dumlin wi po?" she asks, and asks again.
"Dumlin wi po?"
Finally the Caucasian customer understands and nods.
Song Ling is learning English.
She learns from Li Po, who does not know English
But who understands English. He grins politely.
"You must not say 'Dumlin wi po," he says
                                        in Chinese and English sounds.
"You must say, 'Dumplings with pork.' That is what
                                                you must say."
"I will say that," says Song Ling. "Dumplings wi po.
                                        Dumlings wi po."
Li Po grins again.
              "Pork," he says. "Pork. Ka. Ka. Porka."

"Po," says Song Ling. "Po-ka."

Song Ling will learn. She is bright.

Li Po is not the fastest bean snapper in the world,
But he is good and steady, and the beans get done,
Piling up in a vast green pile on the table before him.
All washed, vibrating green,
Waiting for the dark pork gravy to mix with them.
If it were not for Li Po
There would be no roof, no walls, to this building.
There would be no dancing down the street.
Two blocks away, there would be no soup cans in the museum...
No stars in the planetarium...
No top to the Empire State Building...
No subways, no Central Park, no Maid of Liberty.

At three p.m. of a weekday afternoon
                                    Li Po snaps beans.
This humble man who runs New York snaps beans,
And when he is finished, he looks at his great pile of beans,
                                                        satisfied.
Then he looks up at a picture on the wall.
For thirty seconds, Li Po contemplates a golden waterfall.
That is his pleasure. That is All.

The Rivers Of Maine

The rivers of Maine
      are made out of the deepest slate
      and run slow and full of purpose
      down through their courses.
The rivers of Maine are thick
      with the content of their work
Just like the mills of Maine
      are its rivers,
      just as sure are they of their duties.

Sit on the bank of a river of Maine,
      and looking across
      you will see that the river is crowned
      as a graveled country road
      is crowned, the middle
      higher than its banks somehow,
And you will see that river run
      slow and powerful and deep.

It will fascinate your eyes
They will not know whether to stay
      or to follow
      there will be a pull from that
      river of Maine
A pull like a magnet will work
      on your heart.

You will be drawn to roll like that river
Rolling, you will roll your sweet love
      into your embrace
And the baby you make on that shore of that
      river of Maine
Will be rolled in love, and importance, and

deepness and sweetness
And he or she will know where he or she was made,
And when the time comes, where to go,
        and how easy it is to get there.
Life will be full for that small babe,
        Full as the slate-colored river
                That runs to the sea
                Full of life,
                        Bursting with purpose.

Somehow I Got His Sledge

Somehow I got his sledge.
He died at ninety,
Tools undistributed.
We divvied them up.
Somehow, I got his sledge.

Seventeen years it sat in the garage,
Unused, unheeded, unneeded.

Somehow this year we decided
          to put in a walkway.
Somehow the blue Vermont schist stone
          on which our land is borne
                    proved breakable.
Somehow I found that if struck right
Blue walkway stone could be smashed into the right proportions
By a blow or two from a well-aimed sledge.

The stone chips flew like bullets when I hit;
Pelted against the house and garage walls like sleet.

Somehow that sledge was just right
Eight pounds of old iron
On an ancient grey hickory shaft
Reinforced with sticky old black bulldog tape at the head-of-haft,
From some old pre-Duct Tape era.

Somehow suddenly I realized
          that sledge worked just as well
On boulders dug up and recovered
From the gravel bed, the space we lay
For the walkway stones –
These now were great ground boulders

Impossible for three young men together to move at all,
        trying all their sinewy might against the world.

Somehow I found out that by trying right
These huge monoliths too could be destroyed,
Smashed up, heaved into the wheelbarrow,
Trundled up next to the driveway.
And they became a wall.

In a few months they will look like
        they've been there two hundred years or more.
Somehow I am seventy-two years old,
Swinging that sledge like old John Henry,
Carving out a whistling rainbow arc
        that's tied all around my shoulders,
Feeling like a new young man.

Strong magic from that swinging lead;
Magic in that old hickory shaft;
Magic from the days when the sledge was young
        in years. That's older than I am now.
I break the rocks, and I am sudden young.

Sy the Aesthete

he brought honey, apples,

      all good things

brought peace to warring parties

      certitude to those who struggled

he was the placid river

      the sighing of the wind in the pines

brightness   white clouds

           gentle rains

   gladness

      all these things were happy in him

he never met a day he didn't like.

and he knew how to leave when it was time to leave

      he did not beg for life

      but simply went

         when it was time

After the rains, the Meskal daisies come –
Shining in the spring grass, underneath the sun...
Old Ethiopian Song

Meskal Night

Night falls with the setting of the sun
Beyond the western mountains
The streams are deep with winter's run of rain.
Darkness. Dark of night. Soft lavender, dew-dropped night,
Laced with the gleam of new grass
Billowing in the night wind of the past.

A star appears in heaven
And the earth sends back a star;
And later, now, the heavens and the hills are all ablaze.
The streaking, cold-limbed comets of the skies
Unheard, are sizzled in the fry of winter's wood.

The New Year's fires of every farm and town
Are built up high. Bring in the old. Once more,
It's time.
In black night fires glow against the black.

The hills are gone; the valleys gone.
The stars shine as in any other night,
Reflected just tonight upon the hills.
The women roast the meat before their farmhouse doors,
And in the towns the men hurl javelins.
They've done it all before.
Burn in the old, for time will not stand still.
Attract the old to what the future wills.

The MacDougal Plays His Fiddle At The Barn

That night I heard him play song out of the rocks
And music cascaded from the sky
Notes flew like fire from his fiddle
And the Lord of the Clans appeared in the clouds
Seated on his throne of ancient amber.
Nostrils flaring the old chief glared,
And nostrils flared, Dougie set the old man's feet to tapping.
Then the growling of the god caused thunder
And the barn around us rocked with melody
Higher and higher did the music fly
'til sometime in the dawn the stage took fire
And flew the music yonder
To somewhere over hill and dale
And Dougie went up in a flame of music
And left no note behind.

I Loved The Laughter

I loved the laughter of my father's folk,
Attained through years of toil and grime.
The winning satisfaction of a well-turned joke
Or of a rude description, just well-timed.
For they were rough-hewn peasants, they themselves
Sired by an Irishman named Pat who crossed the seas
And settled in a coal patch in the hills
Of eastern Pennsylvania. I'd hear
Them jibe and laugh when work was done;
I'd see them sit around the bar.
Six sons they were and they knew how to laugh
And what to laugh at; sure of that –
The fact of simply making it another day
Still with their lungs filled with the smear of coal.
Because of that, their getting old was redefined.
Born old and cold and getting better as they aged,
For somehow things got better through the years.
Behind their laughing eyes you still could see
The deprivation and the strife. They passed all that
And all their laughter at it down to me.

Part 4

Love Potions

A Medieval Song Of Southern France

If I could take you anywhere
I would fly with you
upon the wings of the snow-white swan
back to the gardens of the Princes
of Pérouges.

There you would sit in the Garden of Love.
There the sun would shine down upon you
and the Prince himself would gaze at you
and listen to your song
and smile.

And there within those ancient courtyard walls
you would breathe the air
of frankincense and myrrh, spices and herbs, roses and lilacs;
And all good things of earth
would come true for you, my Love,
and it would be as you have always wanted it to be
for all the days of the earth.

That is what I would wish for you, my Love –
That is what I would wish...

In The Garden Of The Stone Balloon

night

rain in a place not known

in the garden of the stone balloon

the chess players sit at tables underneath the wide umbrellas
undeterred
by rain
or night
for they are used to being in a place not known.

waitresses full of grace sway slowly,
attend the players' needs which are not many
and they are grateful too for the few pennies that they earn
for they too seem captured
by the slow rain and the slow pace of the players
and the slow pace of the island
and the deep darkness of the night.

it fits.

and it is fitting that
in this quiet garden of the café
known as the Stone Balloon
on this sleeping island in the Caribbean Sea
in the midst of Leeward Islands
in the midst of wilding seas
it is fitting that
there is a place for peaceful people
with souls that rage for combat
within the quiet boundaries of the board.

So then,
the Knight moves toward the Queen,
destroys the King in check
takes up his rightful concubinage
despoils the mighty kingdom
and eventually leaves the scene
to other passing generations
which eventually will include
a fellow who with great accumulated knowledge
will pronounce this pas de deux
as Oedipal behavior
at the very least.

The players at the boards sit still and stare.
Eventually one will lose and one will win.
It means the world to them.

O Swift May Wind

O swift May wind
        from western islands blowing
Now tell me whither
        thou art going
And tell me gently
        and in good time
Why is it that I've adopted
        Keats' rhythm; Shelley's rhyme...
What atoms lurk
        beneath the surface here?
Donne's sonnets? Jonson's cheer?

And what have I to do with these
        old romantic and Romanic Brits,
When I have Celtic singers such as Moore,
        and Yeats
Within my geonomic makeup,
        not to mention the Germanic tribe
That dwells within my cranium,
        all ready to sing, and all cranked up to go
A-warbling 'cross the meadows, through the snow!

Spring

Today is the day all the girls let down their hair.
Everything is undone,
Or rather, never done, unbothered to be done.

Clothes draped over blooming, budding bodies
so casually that
you might suspect
Clothes are not meant to be at all.

It is that kind of day.

It is that day
when warm air from the south
slides up the sunward slopes
of mountain towns

And there are thoughts
of going down
to see the snow-fed stream

To scent whatever promise is there
of Spring.

It Is Not That Easy

It is not that easy to make love
to someone who
you could fall in love with
in an instant
      or already have
      and the two of you
      have eyes that know what you have done
      or are about to do.

The Daring Women Of Maine

So handsome, slim, and beautiful
with their sly and winning smiles
that dare you to approach and ask

why they are smiling. They appear
so predatory, in such a luscious way
as they pass you in the aisles of the local supermarket.

The Kiss

Oh what a surprise, that kiss!
We had known each other for years.
We had watched each other, uninterested, it seems
For all those years
While we went about in our separate,
            yet equal, circles.

So that late afternoon
After our party had come down from hiking the range
And we had all agreed to meet
In this one particular tavern in town
That had a reputation for conviviality,
To put it mildly.
After we had sipped our fill of beer
To swab our dusty throats
With music all around us
And time closing in,
When she and her friends needed
            to head back to Boston
and I and my friends needed to head to Montreal,
with the sun sliding down beyond our beloved hills,
and handshakes and hugs and kisses abounded,
we found ourselves next to one another at the bar.
Drinks finished,
We looked at each other
And perfunctorily hugged
And looked again
And kissed
And startled
Looked into each other's widened eyes.
Stilled for a moment
Then kissed again.
Real kiss, this time.

Again we parted
Unbelieving what we had missed
For all those many years –

A perfect kiss
A perfect fit of lips on lips
Just parted right, just so,
Just right.

And once again we looked into each other's eyes.
Universes. Stars. Unicorns abounded and abounding
       Fourteen-line-stanzas
            Of silver and gold and
                 Diamonds in the night
Blazing stars
Earths moving
Rats!
A perfect fit
       Abandoned unheeded unknown for so, so long

And now,
       No time
           To make it up
                 Forever.

Dream Angel, 1955

I had no idea who she was.
      I didn't know things like this
            could happen.
St. Patrick's Day
      Off Fifth Avenue
            In Central Park
                North of the Museum
Watching the Parade go by before it turned down 86th Street.

Green sparkles glittered on her cheeks
      And with the élan that's special to Manhattan, she
         Kissed me Happy Saint Patrick's Day with ruby-painted New York lips.
            Maybe she was fourteen. I know I was. Startled, I
      Found out that day
         that wonderful sparkling young New York City Irish girls could
         open
              grand new worlds –
      Oh, she was beautiful.
We, both so young, and learning, and alive.

Walk On The Beach

Walk on the beach with me, lass, under the Cruzan moon

Let the silver moonbeams
fall into your hair

Let them sparkle there, and then,

lift your eyes up to the sky
and remember why
I am not there

In the trade winds gently blowing
beneath the brilliant moon

And sigh then,

and remember me.

Part 5

Down to Earth

View From A Hillside Overlooking Lake Champlain

Stand on this hill
and, facing west, then
– stretch out your arms to north and south –

then gaze below them at the length of lake
and look to right and left
and see Champlain stretch well beyond the reaches of your fingertips
until it curls and bends and disappears into the distance.
In olden times, it had a different name.
They called it, then, The Sea Between.

Look now across the lake at Adirondack ranges in the west –
six or seven ranges you can see from here at least
stretch far and further into the dimness of the mist,
and if you look with care, and if you have the gift,
you can see the old gods on the highest ridges of those ranges
brandishing their war clubs and their lances –

But let that vision go.
Look down upon this land that leads down to the lake.
There is a softer, simpler beauty in this land;
a quiet beauty worked into the land like spider's lace.
Below us are the hayfields, some left fallow
for the bobolinks and larks to sing and skylark in.
Before your eyes stand rows of oaks indifferent in their majesty,
then great swaths of forest green – maple, cedar, ash, and
shagbark hickory,
and lower still, bogs quiet in the day
except for froggies tuning up for evening songfests and display,
and scattered all about small houses for the bluebirds
that you see as flashing points of almost neon light.

And all of this grand panorama has been saved
for you and countless other animals and birds
and flowers of the fields and forests and of
mountain bogs and vernal pools.
Go now and take the trail, and ramble round this
saving grace of nature,
this refuge saved for all the future time
that we can see,
this parcel subtle as the earth is long.
All elements rejoice, and raise their souls in song.
Drink in this beauty, bright and deep.
Forever, it is yours to keep.

DUCK! Here Comes the Train!

At midday when the train from Rutland comes
a-flying up the new-laid track
It hums, and hums, and hums, and hoots, and shrugs
and comes on strong
And you can hear it as it grinds along
bringing the cement and oil
to Burlington
Because the hum is in the track, besides the
clickety-clack, clickety-clack
And the whole world moves along with that
and resonates in ears and even in your feet.

Over the hills and far away; over the hills and gone –
the right-of-way still sings its terrible infernal song.
A taking of the land is what it is.
If only for a minute of the day
The power of the rail takes nature's soul away.

But I sit on a bench, hard by the track, that
overlooks a tarn,
and in the quiet of the day I see a calm
deep here inside the darkest woods, after
the freight train's gone.
After the diesel's shudder, after the diesel's moan
the chittering chipmunk comes calling
wondering if I bear a gift of crumbs.
Small warblers flit among the undergrowth
wearing white bellies and gray overcoats
And towhees scratch among the fallen leaves
for lunches of their own that Nature on its own provides.

And then I see a ripple on the water's edge
and then a Wood Duck pops out of the sedge,

propels himself across the pond, quiet as a mouse,
then joined by, possibly, his spouse, and then
four more of them, the males with brightest
colors round their heads, and all of them
intent on quietude.
They do not spy me spying them from my woodland bench,
and I, I watch their quiet paddling
as they go by.
And all of us seem quite content to listen to
the falling leaves of autumn
hit the ground without a sound except
for when they come down from the sky
and hit the curled-up leaves of days gone by.

The Saco At Dahl's Reserve, North Conway

In the spring the Saco roars and tears its way along its ancient bed.
Fed by the fires of the sun, these crystals of the final snows
  cascade down from presidential heights where nothing grows
  but rock and ice and winter.
Its waters carry diamonds in its ripples
  that shimmer in the springtime sun,
  and also boulders, tree trunks ripped
  from savaged banks upstream,
And it can carry danger.

But on a placid summer day like this
With fair breezes blowing all around
It rests, and nodding to the trees
That make their stand upon its sandy banks
It slows, and visits with the forest.

Two kinds of beings, each
With its own sense of time, they greet each other.
Long have these two forces of the earth been neighbors –
The river never knowing time except as headlong rush;
The forest knowing every single year
  inscribed in its concentric circles...
And yet they take one of our aeons
To meet together, before each of them is gone –

The river, turbulently philosophizing where it is,
And where it is going, and whence it came to be,
Until it tumbles to the vastness of the sea;

The forest, glowing silent in its green,
Crumbling placidly into the mists of time
But leaving something of itself behind.

And yet, they speak, or meet at least.
On this fine day enjoying, the two of them together,
Everything about the earth
Under the sun of summertime.

Part 6
The Best of Critters

Cicada

The carapace splits,
Breaking the cicada's back.
Music fills the air.

Monarchs Of The Realm

The Monarchs fly in spring and fall;
In spring, they're hardly seen at all,
But in the fall, they flutter by
And look like oak leaves as they fly,
Or like a wing of areoplanes
They swoop down from their high domains
From thermal lifts of mighty length
And light on milkweed, gain their strength,
Then up into the sky they go
To get far south before the snow,
And powered by the goldenrod's sweet nectar
They'll not be seen again this year, if ever.
But they will still their destinations plot
And end up where it's nice and hot.

Twilight Of The Frogs

The symphony of frogs starts up in the Spring
When the Chorus Frogs begin to sing,
And these are followed by the piercing violins
Of Peepers, yes, Spring Peepers, that sing the springtime in.
The Wood Frogs, woodwinds, gronk their monosyllables amain;
And Tree Frog piccolos are heard this springtime once again.
Staccato Leopard Frogs are all the rage
As their percussion section takes the stage;
While Green Frogs come upon the stage so late
They must tune up – their single strings vibrate.
American Toads, high up in the trees,
Sing such shrieking sopranos you'd hardly believe they
Didn't come from some kind of jungle cat, or maybe a baboon,
And Bullfrogs chime in with tubas and bassoons.
Harrumph! Harrumph! Harrumph di di aye yi yi yi yi
Harrumph! Harrumph! Harrumph di di aye yi yi yi yi
And on into the night this cacophony does ring:
Exuberating exhilarants exhilarating sing!
Let's hope this stays, this twilight of the frogs,
And does not portend the twilight of these woodland gods.

Garth The Big

Oh, Garth the Big was a mighty fine pig
With a mighty fine curlicue
On his mighty fine tail. When he'd give it a whirl
He could stir up quite a stew

With a hint of mischief in his bright blue eyes
He'd wink, give a grin or two
And an 'Oink!' would emerge from deep below,
Somewhere near his heart, just for you.

For Garth the Big was a big-hearted pig;
Had a heart that was true-blue
And one fine day in the merry month of May
Garth met a young sow named Sue
Who was destined to become the grandmother of one
Great big pen of piglets. It's true!

Well Sue took the heart of that big wild boar
And turned him into a puddle
Of blubbering pathos enlaced with bathos
And blithering porcine stew.

"Oh, won't you come gambol and snarfle with me?"
Said Garth the Big to Sue —
"I can see you like edibles sloppy and wild,
Like mushrooms and acorns and beechnuts too.

"I know a spot where pig dreams are born.
It's up on that hill in the forest.
We'll feast on chanterelles, that rhymes with bells
That will play on our wedding day,

"And there we'll stay, wile the summer away,
Midst the walnuts and hazelnuts, too,
And fungo porcino and champignons
With shitakes, enokis, and portobellos
And morels, and hen-of-the-woods, woo-hoo!

"And if we are lucky, my sow young and plucky,
We may snuffle around and root out of the ground
Some funky and muskkevous black truffles, too.
A paradise we'll find, my one Sue sublime
This is my promise to you."

And to this day, they oink away
In perfect pig bliss and true,
And coming in spring, while bluebirds sing,
A litter of piglets for two.

Bullfrog

There's a fine old bullfrog back down there in the pond
      down the hill, beyond the old stone wall
that marks the boundary of the field
      and the wooded hillside that I'm on.
I hear his garumph garumph garumphing all the solstice night,
      while fireflies light up the woods,
          trying to glint their cold cold fire light
            off his tough hide.
But hide he will, and hide he does,
      from the pterodactycally great blue heron
          that searches the shore
            and looks and croaks and looks and looks
              for more and more and more.

And that is his life-cycle as he sings
      his garumph garumph garumphing song.
It isn't long, but longer
      than the other froggies in the pond. At least
He gets to hop on some good-lookin' girl frog's back
      And hump. Before he burrows in the mud,
He has his one last pre-fall pre-frost fling.
      "Winter or the heron's bill, or bliss" he sings, and sings, and
      sings;
All through the summer night, he sings.

Bees

The bees are on their knees, they say,
But their hives are full of honey.
They toil and buzz throughout the days –
That's how they make their money.
They're just like us in many ways,
They store up all they make, sir,
But when the winter's said and done
They're out again – see how they run
About the surface of their hives.
Their buzzing wings say 'Strive!' 'Survive!'
But still the toxins do attack
And strive bees might, but they do lack
The armaments to fend the toxins off.
We must protect them at all costs
And strive ourselves, come with our aid,
Or we, too, humans, dig our grave.

Willing To Listen

There is a real knack
      in being willing to listen
Just today on my walk
      I met a turtle who was
            just beginning to cross the road.

"Say", I said – it was a beauty of a turtle,
      a painted turtle, just in the prime
      of its life, spots on claws and neck
      and head gleaming,
      carapace too gleaming in the noontime sun.

      "Say", I said – it had just taken one
      turtle-length stride out onto the road,
      then felt me coming along
      and hissed up most of the way
      into its shell.

"Say," I said, "Aren't you heading the
      wrong way? The stream bank's back
      along the way you're coming from."

The head protruded slightly from its shell,
      the neck unfolding.

"I'm not going near that stream again
      for another month," it said.
"It's been over its banks five times
      in the last two weeks.
      Weather's changing, I'm afraid,
            Too damn tumultuous for me, at any rate.
            I'm heading for that pond across the road;
            Sit out the weather change from there."

"That pond's at least a half-a-mile away,"
        I said. "You'll dry out half-way there.
                The stream is right down there, back there."
I picked him up. He squirmed out of his shell,
        Raking the air with anxious claws. I held him high,
                Turned him around. Put him down on the ground again.
        He galloped into the weeds –
                Well, lurched, is what he did,
        But he probably thought of it as galloping.
                Whatever,
        In a few gallops he had disappeared
                Into the roadside weeds
Which were uncut because the road crew
        was too busy putting town roads back together
                after all those damned storms
                        to cut any roadside weeds.

But I was satisfied.

He was lurching back toward the stream, last I'd seen.

        I walked on.
A hundred feet down the road
                I turned around.

There he was, heading across the road again,
        once more in the direction of the far-off,
                possibly unattainable forever pond.

Some people are just never willing to listen.

The Beaver

The beaver, you know, he runs the whole show,
Like any good carpenter does,
First his logs he retrieves, from the bank and the leas,
And smacks them together with mud.
And his pond he then fills, and it fills with bluegills,
Or, with any luck, some kind of trout.
And his home he then builds, with all kinds of frills,
(not the least is the hidden way out)
And his larder he fills, with the branches he mills,
And delectable watercress sprouts.

Then the pond it fills up with all kinds of stuff
Like salamanders, amphibians, and such
Who feed on the larvae of mayflies
And other incredible bugs.
And whirligigs whirl and hellgrammites curl
And the nymphs and the naiads do flourish
Then burst through the surface into summer's air
Where they're suddenly seen as if in a dream
To become ancient damsels and dragons,
And they fly through the air and zoom everywhere
In an absolute frenzy of tag-ons.

Well, while all this is happening, the deer comes to drink,
Along with the bear who stands on the brink
And the otters come, too, along with the shrew,
And the turtle suns on her log
And eyes the fox who is licking his chops
And wondering what mischief to do.
While high up above, the eagle she soars,
And the swallows, while flying much lower,
Collect their dinners of surfacing swimmers
Intent on a season of glory, or more.

Meanwhile Missus Beaver is carrying pups
And showing them just how to gnaw their way up
To adulthood, and then they depart
To start their own pond just upriver
From the folks back at home,
And with sleek coats do roam
In search of their own pond and dinner.

And so, dear reader, you see the importance
Of beavers in our ecology.
If it weren't for beavers, there would be no spring
For so many species, and what would become of diversity?
Would it go up in a forest of flame,
Or come down in a deluge of rain,
With icebergs on fire, midst nuclear mire, and
other scenarios dire?
Or shall we esteem a new world serene,
All held together by a beaver regime,
And thanks to this builder and striver,
The Earth, blue and green,
Will still be our home forever...

The Bobcat

The bobcat that runs down the lane
Takes off like a shot, might and main
Grabs a rabbit or two
Enough for a stew
And thus she completes the food chain.

Can There Be Panthers About?

Within the realm of predatory beasts, from weasel up to eagle
We have here represented all of them, from bear and fox to beagle
But there is one we cannot count, for there have been no sightings,
The mighty catamount is out, and counted just in 'mightings.'

Elegy For A Spring Squirrel

Squirrel, I have not seen such courage in a long, long time.
How you got to the side of Hollow Road I do not know.
Knocked out of a tree; sideswiped by a car –
The means of your death means nothing.
The manner of your death, everything.
You knew your death was coming.
You crawled to a place safe from the thundering cars.
You curled up in a circle of repose, your
       Paws against your chest,
       your head tucked against
       your breast.
No king in all of Christendom or out of it
Ever looked better on his bier,
And you did not need the accoutrements we use
To indicate your dignity.
You did it alone,
Alone with God and Universal Death.
Repose was in your soul,
       waiting to come out.
It came. You went.
So may we all, with such sweet beauty.

Sunlight And Magic Stars

sunlight and magic stars

        silver feathers

             wings of gold

all the delights that Earth can hold

           sunlight and magic stars

sunlight and magic stars

             peace and quiet

     thunder   lightning

          all in between are ours

sunlight and magic stars

        golden feathers

             wings of silver

round and round they go

          fractured in zodiac signs

still all is sublime

       sunlight and magic stars

        time is unbroken

Part 7
Phenomena of the Aged

Marblehead

I have written this day in Marblehead
At a sea-captain's desk in a well-furnished inn
On a nor'easter day of wettest gray
Around the corner from the sea
Where the waves boom high at Castle Rock
And the spume sprays heaven above my head.

If I had my choice of a summer's day
With the bluest sky and the whitest clouds
Or this April day with the pounding waves
I'd choose this day when seasalt crystals
Cling to my sweater, my cap, and my beard
And the wind drives the rain into my eyes.

I'd thus have seen the sight I need
To know the sea and what it can do
When its mind is made up, and it has a mind
To be itself in its tough-and-tumble.

The Fall Of Autumn

When Joanie called me down from upstairs
To watch the local turkey herd run 'cross our lawn,
I came down quicker than expected, shoeless.
Turning to accommodate the landing of the stairway,
Something, don't know what it was, went wrong,
And suddenly the world was spinning all too fast
And somewhat upside down.
I caught a glimpse of Joanie's smiling face
Turning from happiness to horror as I fell
Then in no time at all I saw
The lamp base coming up towards me
"Oh, shit," was all I could think out
Before my head slammed into metal –
Saw the flash – not stars – just one big bright lightning bolt –
Then all went black, but not for long.

I tried to move my head. It moved,
So figured out I had not broke my neck;
Then moved my left arm. Yeah, that moved,
So was not broken, either. I tried my legs,
My right arm pinned beneath me,
I still upside down, of course. You see
All kinds of things quite differently from
That perspective. Raised my left arm,
Grabbed the near arm of the couch, with Joanie
Shouting in my ear, "Don't move!" good nurse
That she was. Bad patient that *I* was,
Determined to get up, I started up the side
Of the couch, grabbing hold like a vast
And bulbous arachnid out of the depths of
My imagination. Hauled myself up to a kneeling
Position, then stood up, horrifying her, who said
"Sit down!" "Toe hurts," I said. "Big toe." And then I

Sat, she looking down on me, and I said, "Gimme a drink."
Which surprisingly, she did. And surprisingly, I
Did not spill it, either.

That was on Wednesday afternoon. Today I still feel
Somewhat like the Irishman who fought the barrel of bricks
To a standstill, the barrel landing on top of him.
But healing nicely, I presume. No concussion evident yet,
At least. But pretty stiff, though. The broken toe
Is blue. The rug burn still not healed by any means.
The whole right side feels stretched by a giant chiropractor.
I feel the same as Torrey Carpenter felt during the
Notre Dame – Texas game, when he got whipsawed by
Two Texas thugs. Excuse me if I hobble around somewhat.
Still getting newly used to things.
There goes another life for this old cat.

At The Seaside Resort

He sits beneath a woman's hat.
Its brim is wider than a mile.
It reflects sunlight back to space.
Its strap secures a jagged smile
From this old man who once was whole
And vibrant, juicy, fierce, and bold;
But now, due to a stroke of luck,
Sits quietly and rests, dumbstruck.

I Never Used To Be Afraid Of Sharks

Standing on a yellow
thick-sand ocean beach
at dawn
Looking out over the calm and
scarcely-swelling sea
that looks no more like sea
than thick grey soup

Watching the light change in the
east, the earth
preparing for the sun,
The flat sea waiting to turn
emerald green, topaz, bronze, azure

The breeze the slightest
breeze you ever knew

I wondered what bellowed
just beneath the placid
surface

And I decided that for once
I would not simply
just barge in,
slipping my bulky landbody
in between the molecules of
wave
silently
like a wraithe.
No. This time I stopped and wondered
what sandpaper-armored
gray-white body

lurked for me below those placid waters
watching for its morning meal.

I never used to be afraid of sharks.

Now I am older, and wary of
a death that lurks
unnecessarily beneath the surface
of any new endeavor.

The Grizzly

No more will I fight the Grizzly;
No more will I fight the Bear.
Last night, at dusk, seated on my deck,
I heard the footsteps in the leaves
Ever so stealthily climbing the wooded hill
       behind my house.
I sat and waited.

I had spent the afternoon rooting up weeds
      from the perennial garden
I had spent the day trimming the mock orange back,
      preparing for fall.

These things I could fight to a standstill,
      but... the Bear?

These things took my strength.
No longer had I need to be agile.
No longer did I need great fury.

After those little tweaks in the heart region –
Twice in one week, and one a month ago –
Now I knew that if I fought the Bear
It would be no contest.
Bear would have knocked me ass over teakettle
Into the flowers and branches and weeds
      I had carefully left unraked.

      Sprawled across the lawn,
When I rose to my knees
Bear would have given me just one swift swat –
Unless my aging heart, by giving out,
Would drop me first into the grass.

No, peering at eighty through the gloom of dusk,
Gratified for the deer it was that scampered away,
No longer would I hope for bear or dragon.
No longer need I much adventure.
Now I need to say to all who might so wish to listen,

"Now I no longer fight the Bear.
Now I wait for the Great Bear –
The one who comes for us all in the end;
Now I raise my eyes unto the stars
Looking for the Light that comes for all of us."

Voyage

My stateroom is empty.
I am at sea
Alone, in a grand ship,
I gaze out the porthole:
A bright day, a breeze,
Whitecaps to the horizon.
The gulls wheel for me.
My stateroom is empty.

Part 8

Fare Thee Well

Bright Star

I was so happy that year,
when we spent the summer on the southern isle.
Every day we watched the sun rise.
Seated on the top of the cliff
next to the rough-barked cedars
we looked out over the Inland Sea,
our arms around each other;
And every morning I put my hands on your belly
        to measure it.
Then we would sit and laugh
        and have contests, just the two of us,
         and bet on when the baby would be born.

At the end of July it was.
On a morning fresh with the beads of dew, I, waking early,
        saw Orion ranging over the horizon to the east,
           along with the pre-dawn light.
Stealthily, with no noise, I picked up my shotgun and bow
        and crossed in my moccasins away across the land.
Beyond our campsite, far away,
I sat beneath a maple tree on the side of a field,
and waited.

Silence. An hour's wait. Silence.

Just at the edge of daybreak
an old Tom Toddler tippled into the field,
falling out of some sumac scrub.
He went about his business
scratching away for all he was worth,
roaming towards me,
and I –

I blasted him.
Picked him up by the neck.

Carried him home,
lifted up the blanket
that was the door to our tent,
And I stood there, silent and amazed.

You were turned away from me.
Naked, you knelt on bunched blankets,
your black hair cascading down your ivory back,
and when you heard me enter at the door
you turned your head
and with a smile, said,
"While you were away, she came."

I will take the curve of your mouth,
Your smile, your gleaming eyes,
          forever with me.
To my grave, I will take the beauty of you
          on that day, with me.
Every day I wake, I will take the look of you
          on that day, with me.

"See," you said, and turned around to me, smiling.
At your breast was a delicate thing
with delicate lips, and delicate fingers,
and bright black eyes.
"Aiyee!" I said.
I saw your questioning lips, and then you said softly,
"Come look." You stopped, and looked at me,
          and smiled again, and said,
"But leave the turkey outside."

I looked down.
I, great hunter, had brought you a dead turkey,
with eXes for eyes, and buckshot aplenty
in his wings and breasts and thighs.
And while I was about that,
You brought me an angel.

How is that?
Am I not the great provider?
Am I not the great hunter?
So how did you deliver this bright beauty?
All alone, how did you do this
while I was out sitting under a tree
in the still dimness of the green dawn?
"What can I do?" I asked, and knew
        there was nothing I could do.
"Be happy," you said.
"There must be something I can do," I said.
"Bring me a pot," you said. "I will need strength.
 We will make a soup out of your buckshot turkey."
"I do not know how to....." I said.
"Oh, I will do it," you said, "...and you will pluck the feathers."
"I?" said I.
"Aye," you said.

"And what shall we call this miracle?" I asked.

"She came just before dawn," you said,
"She came with the morning star.
"We should call her, 'Bright Star'".

"That is good," I said.

"Build up the fire and start the soup," you said.

I knelt, hand upon your strong young back, and
        watched Bright Star. She went to your
        nipple, mewed, sucked, drank in your milk,
        drank in the summer day.

Outside, birds sang. Waves splashed against the
        shore.   A quiet morning.
            No other sound.

The Last Great Poem Of Earth

The last great poem of Earth
Blasted off into space today;
Roared up from the Western American Desert
Riding up on its afterburners,
Holding onto its arc for dear life,
Hurtling away through the stratosphere
On a pillar of white smoke and orange fire,
Scattering the air apart,
Space dirt and dust wafting down in its wake.

Over and up and out over the Southwest it went
On its way to the celestial skyway
The mighty heavens
The unknown orbit
That flies around until it finds
The Universe, and the place
Where that place meets Infinity.

Off it went,
Over the Natural Bridges,
Engines aglow –
Full throttle –
Full one hundred mach speed ahead –
Carrying with it
The flute songs of Taos Pueblo,
The silver of Santa Fe,
Jack Kennedy's smile,
Charlie Chaplin's walk,

Blue sky, white cloud –
And Christ and Buddha sat up on a mesa top,
And watched it go.
Necks craned back,
Eyes to the skies,
Teeth bared in gleaming grins,
Delighted, they laughed.

What The Abenaki Say About Dogs

The Abenaki say this:
When you pass over
To the next abode,
You rise from your dream
And walk through the forest.
A long trail you walk.
It is pleasant, with trees
That rise above you
And leaves and moss
Soft beneath your moccasins.
Then you come to a river...

Over the river there is a bridge.
On the bridge stand all the dogs
You have ever known in your life.
If you have treated them well
They greet you as they have in life
And walk with you across the bridge
Into the light of the next life.

If you have not treated them well,
You will never cross that bridge.

The Primitive's Grave Barrow At Avebury

Old bones grow cold.
I wish mine, then,
To have some sun and air
A view of mountains
A sight of the sea
Reminders of the earth's great curve.

Above me, for a blanket, thick-wove wheat.
Some charcoal situated in my green-baulked house
   would make a welcome hearth –
Finally, a fruit tree of some kind nearby.
And make sure that either I, or just the place itself
Align properly and prominently with one, thus two, of
    the great directions –
This is most important, and advantageous to
    a good deep dream sleep.
And again, then,
This kind of virtuous and loving care
Also aids the great awakening.

Oh, and put my arrows there.
And my bow,
And my fishnet.
And my music.

~with thanks to the many who have helped me along the way ~

Besides Joan Bowker, my darling companion for nigh-on 50 years, to whom this book is dedicated...

My mother, who read children's poems to me, and occasionally threw in a quatrain from Shakespeare...

Professor William McBrien of St. John's University, extraordinary master of 17th Century Metaphysical Poetry, and the other professors of the English Department, especially Drs. Johnson, Kunkel, Holland and Franzetti...

The denizens of the Gaslight Café on MacDougal Street in Greenwich Village, including Jack Kerouac, Allan Ginsberg, John Brent, Hugh Romney (Wavy Gravy), Dave Van Ronk, and especially Buffy Sainte-Marie...

The Calypsonians and Druzbans of St. Croix, U S Virgin Islands...

The members of the League of Vermont Writers, especially Pat Goudey O'Brien, Paula Diaco, Ted and Marie Tedford, Jerry Johnson, and Sharon Faelton...

Pat Goudey O'Brien deserves a separate mention. As publisher of Tamarac Press, she is responsible for the development of three of my works: *Song of Quebec*, *The Glory of the Kings*, and *What the Abenaki Say About Dogs*. Thank you, Pat!

Reviewer K.R. of 7 Days...

The members of the Poetry Society of Vermont, especially Ann Day, my mentor through so many years, and George Longenecker, Marta Rijn Finch, Carol Milkuhn, Sarah Dickenson Snyder, Phil Coleman and Cindy Ellen Hill...

Poet Laureate of Maine Baron Wormser, who in an exuberance of enthusiasm, once compared *The Saco at Dahl's Reserve*, *North Conway* and *New Hampshire* with the poetry of Ralph Waldo Emerson (he has since modified his appreciation to 'Emerson-like')...

Donna and John Moody of The Winter Center, an Abenaki self-help agency...

Mary Catherine Jones, Executive Director of VoiceOverVermont, who recorded *What the Abenaki Say About Dogs*...

John Coyne and Marian Biel, editors of Peace Corps Writers, who named *The Glory of the Kings* winner of the best work of fiction 2014...

The members of the South Burlington Poetry Group, especially Lois Bresee, Laura Fontaine, Dan Guertin, Sue Olenek, Lynn Pryer and Yitzi Gittlesohn...

Burlington Writers Workshop...

Sue Smith, Co-Director of the Charlotte Park and Wildlife Refuge...

Margaret Woodruff, Director of the Charlotte Library, and Lori York, Director, and Kerrie Pughe, Coordinator of the Charlotte Senior Center, Vermont...

Lis McLoughlin, Publisher of *Writing the Land*, and Liz Burton-Crowe, its Technical Director, both of whom are the most patient and dogged publishing people I have ever worked with so far (Look up WTL on the web.)...

And finally, Sofia, Rachel, and Kim of Onion River Press and Michael DeSanto, Renee Reiner and Tod Gross of Phoenix Books, Burlington, Vermont, who are right up there with my previous publishers. I know how to pick 'em!

~Thank You All ~

Dan Close is a poet and novelist writing in the hills of northwestern Vermont. Among his works is a volume of poetry entitled *What the Abenaki Say about Dogs* and the novels *Song of Quebec* and *The Glory of the Kings*, winner of the 2014 Maria Thomas Best in Fiction prize from Peace Corps Writers. Another of his works, *Tales from the Arusi Hills*, is held in the Special Collection of Peace Corps Writing at the Library of Congress. His poetry appears in several anthologies. He is currently a member of the Poetry Society of Vermont. You can learn more about Close at his website: danclose.net.